Advice and guidance
for providers of training
and business support

How to
work with
small businesses

Acknowledgements

The ADAPT FESME VCU project partners are indebted to many people who gave their time to assist in creating constructive ways to forge closer community relationships between the FE sector and the small employer sector.

College representatives have assisted in various ways. They responded to the first national survey of college views on working with small businesses in autumn 1998. The project survey also sought views on Ufi and was followed by a national survey that sought views on the new Small Business Service. College representatives also attended events on related issues, including the project's three events during March and April 2000. Special thanks are due to Barnet College, Farnborough College of Technology, Filton College, MANCAT, Gateshead College, Oldham College, Rotherham CAT, Somerset CAT and Stockport College of higher education and further education. These colleges all informed and influenced the project work, as have representatives from many ADAPT projects, including the Marchmont project.

The ADAPT FESME VCU project is also indebted to representatives from small businesses who gave their time in interviews organised through colleges and in representation of membership organisations comprising small businesses across all sectors, and groups of smaller organisations providing specific services, from accountancy through residential care to outdoor recreation.

Lastly, the ADAPT FESME VCU project thanks the TUC, for its interest in encouraging real employment opportunities in a market economy.

Introduction

As the proportion of small and medium-sized enterprises (SMEs) grows, their contribution to the local and national economy becomes more significant. Colleges are keen to co-operate with small businesses for many reasons, including the fundamental one of ensuring that local young people progress successfully, from school to college and into employment. A growing number of colleges recognise that one of the most effective services they can provide to local, small employers, is to liaise with local schools, to raise awareness of career opportunities. However, efforts to communicate effectively with small workplaces may be a marginal activity within a college's endeavours to deliver a broad range of initiatives.

In some regions a high level of collaboration between colleges has secured good penetration of specific services for local businesses. Some colleges have forged successful relationships with local, small businesses on a commercial basis, where the business pays wholly for the services that the college delivers. A much greater proportion of college provision to employees is publicly subsidised, either through delivery of training to recognised standards, like National Vocational Qualifications (NVQs), or through project work, funded for short-term periods of about one to three years. Overall the incidence of partnerships between colleges and small workplaces remains patchy.

This is not due to lethargy or a lack of investment on the part of colleges, but to a series of problems that all providers or services to SMEs face, to varying degrees. Current services offered by providers may not focus on improving small businesses' competitiveness. Colleges may not effectively communicate information on the practical services they offer to employers in specific sectors.

Eligibility criteria for subsidised post-16 training may exclude valuable training to workers in SMEs and non-SME friendly industrial policies raise further barriers. Policies to counter the adverse effects of unbridled 'market economies', e.g. on small businesses' capacity to provide employment have been called for. Professor Frank Coffield and others have noted the need for effective industrial policies which complement education and training policies to:

- upskill the workforce
- transfer responsibility for remaining employable to individuals.[1]

Initiatives that attempt to develop a learning culture in companies feature in the most recent government interventions, including University for Industry (Ufi), with its learndirect brand and learning centres, many of which are run in association with selected colleges. Ufi, as a flagship of the lifelong learning initiative, will only succeed in small workplaces, if national industrial policies are aligned with those promoting lifelong learning.

In the short term, better processes for gathering information on small businesses needs are required and the concept of entrepreneurship and commercial viability needs to be developed, at local and national levels. This is fundamental to the development of SME-friendly systems of national qualification standards and to the design of appropriate training and support services. Radical approaches to improving support to small businesses are essential, so that the sector can continue to play its increasingly valuable role, in sustaining some 55%[2] of the UK's workforce and in providing local jobs.

This publication provides guidance on good practice to help providers improve the quality and relevance of services to SMEs. It also outlines some problem areas requiring policy changes. Without policies that reflect the needs of SMEs and complement education, scepticism[3] about the usefulness of state-instigated training and support services will remain. Such scepticism could depress the learning opportunities by SMEs and limit their involvement in Modern Apprenticeship training.

Key research findings

1 Trading conditions for SMEs

Globalisation and 'best value' procurement cultures can threaten SMEs' viability. Established supply chain relationships may be threatened and lower profit margins may result in downsizing and loss of local jobs. Where new businesses are started, it can take some years before they are sufficiently established to provide sustainable local employment. Where start-ups have been subsidised, this may undercut an established local business, to the detriment of its survival.

Providing support for SMEs in such an uncertain economic climate thus becomes more difficult while this environment cannot be improved solely by services provided by colleges and other agencies. However, to be successful in a knowledge-based economy, SMEs must be clever, nimble and adept at changing to meet new demands and new markets. In an ideal world, a culture that motivates large organisations to place some small value contracts would be instigated. This way more businesses may compete with a higher chance of securing business and being able to sustain jobs in local communities. However, such a major culture change could be deemed counter to competitiveness in national and international terms, and would require reform of international policies, such as those that underpin the European Union's public procurement system.

The unemployment situation would seem to have improved due to the increasing number of people in work in the UK. However, this masks another result of globalisation, in that many of the full-time jobs lost seem to have been replaced by part-time jobs, and by ones with poorer terms and conditions. The Labour Force Survey, on which most job-level statistics are based, only requires a person aged 16 years and over, to have worked one paid hour in a week to qualify as employed. People on government-supported employment training schemes, along with those doing unpaid work in a family business, are included in the employee jobs count. Currently, part-time working is increasing at a rate some four and a half times that of full-time working.[4] Providers of support for SMEs need to be aware of the economic climate in which they operate. Firstly support to the needs of the business, and its continued success in a global market, may be key to the development of effective measures to support local firms.

2 Services on offer

The FEDA ADAPT FESME VCU baseline survey report (1998) asked colleges about their services to SMEs. A wide range of activity was identified, including:

- direct training – provided by 88% of the colleges surveyed
- training on employers' premises
- training using ICT or distance learning
- partnership activity relating to project funding or mutually beneficial developments, such as work placement provision.

However, there are undoubted difficulties for providers and for their clients in seeing an effective match between what SMEs require and what the college can provide. The cost to the small company of purchasing bespoke training may be prohibitive, but regular provision subsidised by the public purse, may be equally inappropriate due to:

- requirement to attend at a specific time on a regular basis
- the need to link learning to whole nationally recognised qualifications (although this requirement has been relaxed recently).

There are other possible variations to what is on offer. Provision may be shared with other companies to secure economies of scale, open and distance learning may be available, although to release public subsidy, these still need to be linked to the achievement of approved qualifications. Many EU-funded programmes offer free needs analysis; support for business planning and development have been available from TECs and Business Links. Despite all of these measures, finding solutions to business problems through learning directly related to SMEs business emphasis is a complex process. For providers, the SME market is also difficult. Significant effort, including expensive and time-consuming relationship marketing is required and financial rewards are small. However, for providers who are committed to improving the economic competitiveness of their local business community, the task is well worthwhile.

3 National training schemes

Without sustainable development, services cannot be planned, marketed and delivered effectively to aid the local community. The lack of well-targeted funding, is exacerbated by the high investment required to make informed judgements about the merits of training options and learning services.[5] Such evaluation is essential so that the benefits of different options may be gauged by:

- colleges, so that they may accurately predict what services to offer
- learners from the workplace, who will be looking for formal development
- employers, who will be concerned about the impact of services on their business.

Unless the benefits of the service are seen to provide a potential improvement for the overall organisation and for the member of its staff who will directly receive the services, the business may not see the value of releasing staff or paying for training.

The evaluation process requires investment, as vocational qualifications may appear to be inpenetrable to the non-specialist. For instance, Modern Apprenticeships require apprentices to gain NVQs to level 3. The NVQ system consists of a range of learning activities and training standards determined by national training organisations (NTOs), and awarding bodies, that even colleges find daunting. To the small business, with little knowledge of the language of training and education, this mass is even more daunting. Confusion is increased as some standards are inappropriate to small workplaces, while potentially useful standards are missing from the current system.

The workplace assessment process is resource intensive and many small workplaces require a high level of assistance to achieve appropriate conformance to bureaucratic requirements. This process may work well in larger workplaces, that employ or contract training specialists, but many small businesses do not have access to such specialists. The benefits to SMEs resulting from having staff with NVQs may also not be immediately apparent.

Various alternatives to NVQs may be offered, e.g. through Open College Networks (OCN). These qualifications can be tailored to the needs of small businesses and allow colleges to respond more rapidly to local needs. However, there is a bewildering array of options which may add to the employer's initial confusion when first gauging benefits of the learning services offered. The value of these qualifications can be difficult to judge, and they may not be readily recognised outside a particular region or by appropriate trade, professional or regulatory bodies.

One English region has invested heavily to establish a co-ordinating body that can make NVQ-related awards for engineering apprentice-ships feasible in any size of engineering company, across its region. The body ensures that engineering employers are aware of apprenticeship-related services provided by specific colleges in its region. The initial investment to establish the body and encourage collaboration between colleges and employers will reap long-term savings, as it reduces previous duplication of developing, supporting and marketing services, by individual colleges within the region. This region recognises the additional investment now required to rationalise and improve its other services. This could be extended nationally to overcome barriers that every region in England and Wales faces to some degree.

Improving the value of qualifications

There is general recognition that without modification and significant support, the NVQ system is not the ideal way of developing competence in SMEs. The Qualifications and Curriculum Authority (QCA) and partners are working to improve the value of NVQs and other vocational qualifications.[6] The development of 'Technical Certificates' which make explicit the theoretical aspects of vocational qualifications, is also being considered.

It is essential that current views from workplaces, especially small ones, are gathered and acted upon, so that existing standards and related processes are adapted to conditions in SMEs. Debate over fundamental issues relating to learning in SMEs is required, including:

- changing the national focus away from assessment and towards learning, by concentrating on learning outcomes, i.e. what a learner should be able to do, on completion of a learning programme

- re-examination of appropriate assessment criteria and flexible assessment options so students may elect to check for themselves that they are ready to progress. Alternatively, they may prefer formal assessment by an external assessor, on completion of parts or whole courses, perhaps to recognised awards based on units of NVQs

- unitisation of qualifications and appropriate relationships between part and full qualifications, with the amounts of learning that can be counted as a unit and the overall qualification. This may enable routine use of some units within many courses. The sizes of the smallest parts of qualifications, and of whole courses which will be publicly funded, also needs to be determined.

The debate may be stimulated by the increase in opportunities to use computers in the learning process, and development of nationally delivered brands, such as Ufi's learndirect.

The extent to which computerised units of foundation education can be easily tailored to enable learners from different workplaces and on different courses to relate easily to their contents needs to be considered.

Influencing reform of vocational qualifications

The debate should also address how the state could acknowledge informal learning, as most people increase their knowledge to some degree at work, without recourse to the formal education system. Workplaces depend upon informal learning to stay in business and sustain livelihoods, although larger workplaces may wish to release their staff for formal learning. The desire to learn informally at work can arise from many motives, from wishing to maintain a safe and fair workplace through to needing to avoid non-conformance to regulatory requirements. If such informal learning is not acknowledged, initiatives could seem very out of touch with workplace realities and thus fail to be beneficial, especially to those in small workplaces.

Some colleges offer qualifications and awards, sometimes as formally assessed parts of NVQs. It is often far more useful for SMEs to be able to gain access to small chunks of learning, underpinned by national standards. However, care must be taken to ensure part qualifications are adequately maintained to reflect current commercial realities.

Awards covering foundation study on rigorous technical processes are increasingly of interest to small businesses, as their younger staff need to gain greater understanding of fundamental aspects of their jobs. Such progression awards can form parts of apprenticeship schemes.

These awards can also be used by colleges to attract young people who have become excluded from the education system. This should be welcomed but with two riders:

- Appropriate support for students is provided, so they may sustain themselves during the course and successfully re-enter the transition from education to work.
- New awards must be properly promoted to employers; otherwise the chances of the award being valued by employers are reduced.

Effective promotion of the NVQ system at a national level needs to be put in place. The transition from school to college and then to gainful employment is much improved where professional and industrial bodies acknowledge NVQs as recognised routes in the career-related structures that they maintain. Vocational qualifications should also be properly promoted to employers and individuals, and their value agreed and recognised within the industry.

Colleges are well placed to influence reform of national qualifications, as they deliver learning leading to these qualifications direct to small workplaces. Colleges already collaborate with local and regional bodies, including parts of their region's development agencies and Training and Enterprise Councils (TECs) and Business Links (to be replaced by the learning and skills councils (LSCs) and the Small Business Service (SBS) respectively). They may also collaborate with regional parts of national organisations, including Ufi and NTOs.

Feedback from SMEs

Obtaining feedback from SMEs on completion of delivery of their services is becoming routine, and can stimulate the recipient of the services to consider any benefits gained. Providers should avoid superficial methods, however, which supply more comfort to the provider than illumination of the usefulness of services to workplace competitiveness. Reform of qualifications and services, and of their funding mechanisms requires meaningful input from small businesses. Resources for this work could be linked to the production of reports and analysis from SMEs, with due safeguard to ensure this is impartial, meaningful, and impacts on future practice. Findings should be fed back to the appropriate regional and national bodies. Views on difficulties that curb the success of work with small businesses also need to be reported to the appropriate regional and national bodies: perhaps with suggestions for resolving these.

In turn, national and regional bodies should use their power to instigate reform in response to the views received.

4 The need for more information

Impartial information on small businesses' views and practical needs is essential to the development of effective, local services. Poor questionnaire design that has lacked adequate impartiality, coupled with a lack of motivation or resources to research the few sources of impartial information that are available nationally, may have contributed to misinterpretation of SME's views.

Academics and researchers should ensure circulation of their findings and bring forward extracts of previously published reports. New publications have great value as briefing materials, and in the excellent basis they can provide for comparison purposes, to measure changes in small businesses' needs. Web-based information may be of great use in the future.

Robust findings on small businesses' views would assist all who wish to support local employers. A national initiative to raise awareness of such findings would be very effective, particularly if anyone starting on public-funded projects to work with small businesses, was automatically issued with these details. This would both raise awareness and avoid wasting public funds through duplication of effort.

Deepening the understanding of entrepreneurship

If entrepreneurship development is the understanding of how to 'make it easier to start and run a small business', those who are responsible for designing and selling services need an understanding of entrepreneurship and business acumen. This understanding is necessary to achieve effective communication between small businesses and providers of support. Lack of this understanding may have motivated some colleges to focus their resources on the readier target of larger businesses, to the exclusion of small local ones. However, as the proportion of SMEs grows and the numbers of large companies decline, this is no longer a viable option.

Colleges' understanding of entrepreneurship and commercial ethos is rising. Many colleges have established dedicated services for SMEs through business development units or have set income or volume targets for departments relating to work with employers. However, all local providers need to ensure that there are co-ordinated approaches to the same pool of local employers, so that services are offered on the same commercial basis and multiple requests are avoided.

Colleges' understanding of commercial sensitivity is also rising, because of their increased work with firms of all sizes. Colleges are now more aware of the need to retain business confidentiality in a market economy.

Some colleges also note that they may have to work hard to overcome poor perceptions of colleges in small businesses. These negative perceptions may stem from experience of ill-thought through support, which is of little added value and poorly managed. The problems due to lack of added value are compounded when there are inadequate resources to address variable availability and quality of services. A series of such national brands, some delivered by colleges and some not, have left a legacy of unhappy experience. Negative experience of compulsory education and poorly delivered and costly training by colleges is a further contributary factor to poor perceptions.

Defining and measuring competitiveness

Techniques to measure improvement in competitiveness are not commonly understood by business support agencies or policy makers. Without this understanding and those of productivity and profit measures, the design of effective regulatory systems, national training systems and business support services all become subject to chance.

Productivity

In simple terms, productivity may be measured by the ratio of output over input. Production, a term often used mistakenly for productivity, is only one of the output elements, albeit an important one. 'Employee costs', form part of the input. Investment resource is another input element. Productivity ratios and indices may be improved by increasing the output relative to the input, or conversely, worsened by increasing the input relative to the output.

Productivity can also be seen in the wider context of social inclusion. For instance, the resource invested in lifelong learning initiatives, such as ADAPT (an 'input'), needs to achieve an increase in productivity through, for instance, the number of jobs it helps to create or protect ('an output'). Many earlier partnerships failed to deliver 'outputs' in terms of jobs, despite improving collaboration between public-sector delivery agents.

The key issue in building provision of assistance for microbusinesses is that it takes a great deal of investment, in capital terms and in long-term relationships with local employers and communities. Colleges and support agencies may already have made an investment including:

- developing courses to enable learners to accumulate credit towards recognised qualifications
- nurturing collaborative and partnership arrangements, which increase the effectiveness of provision to local employers and employees
- improved internal online systems or enhanced marketing work, for instance, constructing websites with partners or developing electronic course directories
- opening Outreach centres to enable more convenient learning
- employing and developing staff with appropriate skills for SMEs and for training trainers, advisers, mentors, tutors and assessors for SMEs, perhaps within specific industries
- integrating ICT into the supply of assistance to SMEs
- software materials and collaborative development of new materials.

The definition of local competitiveness is also fundamental to the design of effective local support services.

Defining the value of a service

While many small businesses have no training budgets, this should not be interpreted as a lack of interest in training. Instead, providers need to focus on how they can help small organisations gauge the benefits of services in terms of:

- its strategic value
- the improvement in some specific operational details.

For example, to gauge the value of someone in a small business taking a course in marketing; the strategic decision needs to have been made to enter new markets or to penetrate current markets better and the person undertaking the proposed training course needs to believe that it will improve specific operational tasks relating to market research or marketing.

The small business will only purchase the course, and support its member of staff by releasing them during working hours, if both levels of potential benefits are accepted. If the course goes ahead with neither or only one level of potential benefit accepted, then there is a high chance of delivering an unsatisfactory and ineffective service.

5 National backing

The best-established learning services by colleges to small businesses may be those backed by national initiatives or legislative change. Two examples where colleges have penetrated the small business sector are:

- computer-related services, e.g. 'how to use a computer' or 'how to use the e-mail system'
- courses to aid the understanding of regulatory details, like health and safety requirements.

Computer-related activity sometimes termed Information and Communication Technology (ICT), is often financed directly by short-term project funding, in addition to national initiatives on various related issues, such as e-commerce, e-business and e-learning.

The health and safety regulatory requirements are backed by practical guidance from the Health and Safety Executive and local authority environmental health departments. This helps to reduce the investment needed by those designing support services, which are effective in helping small businesses.

A practical focus

Some national initiatives would be improved by a clearer focus on practical details.

It can be difficult harnessing ICT-related initiatives to improve he performance of small businesses. Some ICT initiatives seem to be aimed at people in educational establishments or government departments and for those organising regional infrastructures to deliver centrally determined policies. However, if these result in greater efficiency of regulators' work and of regions' support to business, then small businesses may benefit indirectly, perhaps by better access to improved information sources.

Small businesses may also benefit from using community computer facilities, for instance, in a learning centre located in a high street and run by a college, so that users become familiar with e-mail, or can access library resources on the internet. There are a lack of ICT-related initiatives that could benefit small businesses directly by:

- generating facilities, like computerised learning resources to improve the control of their businesses or processes
- funding practical applications of cultural changes, like e-commerce and e-business.

This lack of initiatives has been a problem area. However, many new initiatives are now geared to provide more of this type of support.[7]

Raising schools' awareness of career opportunities

Some initiatives are instigated by colleges at their own cost. For example, some colleges have noted that local, small businesses have difficulty recruiting new staff and recognise that one of the best services the college can provide is promoting particular career opportunities in local schools. There is no earmarked funding for colleges or small businesses to undertake school liaison, at a time when the need for such work is growing in various sectors, particularly manufacturing and engineering. In the past, large businesses supported national awareness raising opportunities in their specific sectors, but currently most large companies in the engineering, defence, aerospace and manufacturing sectors focus solely on their own businesses.

Need for guidance on employment issues

A major problem faced by employers is the lack of timely and practical guidance on employment issues. Employers need explicit assistance to expand their workforces, and to understand productivity improvement, job evaluation and equitable payment-reward. An understanding of basic workplace techniques is essential, particularly when a business is set up or has to reorganise how it works, e.g. to successfully introduce and maintain the National Minimum Wage; comply with the 48-hour limit within the Working Time Regulations; or deal with the comprehensive provisions within the Employment Relations Act.

The DTI's guidance *Employing staff: a guide to regulatory requirements*,[8] indicates many aspects which must be understood before employing staff, but does not address either the staffing threshold that triggers compliance for some employment laws or basic techniques required to introduce employment laws successfully. The knowledge of requirements over every compliance threshold is critical. For example, businesses that aim to grow to over 20 staff need to understand the processes by which their staff can assert their right to instigate worker representation, within the provisions of the Employment Relations Act 1999.

There needs to be a link between the DTI's policies to increase businesses' productivity and competitiveness and those of the DfEE and NTOs, in particular with regard to work-based training and to national training standards. Small businesses do not have time to lobby their industry-specific NTO to influence the work of generic NTOs. Therefore the messages, for example, that small businesses need to gain basic knowledge to alter their employment practices do not get across.

Another aspect that remains ambiguous to employers and therefore to their support providers, relates to the criteria that a business should invest in, to have the best chance of supplying a large purchaser. For instance, a purchaser may only consider prospective suppliers that are incorporated companies or those that have charitable status. Neither *Setting up in business: a guide to regulatory requirements* nor *Tendering for government contracts* contains guidance on qualification criteria.

Both supplier criteria regulations and employment-related issues are of crucial importance to the establishment and growth of viable SMEs. So too is information on these issues.

Barriers raised by short-term project funding

Colleges are achieving favourable results from work to improve services to local small businesses through short-term projects supported by public funds. These funds come from the UK and from the EC, including its European Social Fund (ESF). However, there are common problems that limit the effectiveness of such projects including:

- Projects are expected to duplicate initial effort, to become familiar with official policies, e.g. on post-16 training and education and on small business support, and to overcome technical limits, for instance, in connectivity and bandwidths.
- Little reliance can be placed upon employment-related statistics.
- Significant resources are required to forge partnerships in bid preparation and bureaucratic administration, as many projects stipulate collaboration as a condition of approval.

- Where short-term project funding is secured to fund learning services, it can be difficult to sustain the project's work in the long term. Project funding to support free services may have inbuilt disincentives to generating income from selling services during the project's lifetime. This helps to enforce proper use of publicly funded awards, but fails to allow a period of transition to implement a culture of charging for services that were initially free. Even if great effort is made early in a project's lifetime to sustain the source after the funding has closed, it may not be feasible to secure the level of resource needed to enable the work to continue. This may be a root cause of a culture of 'project-dependency', that can be counter-productive and time-consuming.

Perhaps as a direct result of the barriers outlined above, some colleges note that private businesses have creamed off the more profitable training provision. The four good practices outlined in the second part of this book are designed to aid colleges in their communications with local, small workplaces: good communications being a fundamental prerequisite to forging good working relationships.

6 Involving trade unions and others in new ideas

Although the confrontational role of the trade unions has changed, some unions remain wary of taking the initiative in assisting small businesses in their protection of jobs, as such assistance may be misread as being a direct approach solely to increase their membership rolls. Examples of ways in which some unions are overcoming this, are as follows:

- Some unions, with members in the arts and broadcasting sectors, are motivated to play an increasing role in resolving small business related issues, as their members' employers have required their contractual arrangements to be changed, from core employment to term contracts or self-employment. A key aspect of the unions' work for these members, has been the development of training services which are available to their members nationally, but which are accredited and supported by only a few, regionally based providers. This aspect of the unions' work has set a precedent for other nationally available services to small businesses.

- Some unions recognise the sense of harnessing overlapping national initiatives to bring multiple benefits for their members, e.g. by producing computer-based earning packages on computers that combine the function of raising basic awareness of computers with that of raising basic literacy or numeracy skills.

If partnerships at work are to be successful in meeting common and mutually agreed objectives, it is essential that training is provided specifically for this purpose. Training would broadly be in two parts:

- the principles of a partnership arrangement
- the specifics of joint working exercises, using appropriate techniques to achieve key and common objectives of real and sustainable performance improvements without recourse to job loss or job degradation.

Competitiveness can be improved through practical initiatives in local workplaces. Trade unions could be most effective in bringing a fresh approach to competitiveness and productivity issues.

The recent changes to employment-related initiatives and legislation provide a timely opportunity and catalyst for effecting positive change and avoiding the pitfalls of some past legislation and practices. Such changes include:

- Welfare to Work and the New Deal
- the Working Time Regulations and The National Minimum Wage
- the Disability Discrimination Act 1995, with its recent amendments
- the Disabled Persons' Tax Credit and Working Families' Tax Credit
- Fairness at Work initiatives, now within the Employment Relations Act 1999.

The regulations in the Employment Relations Act are wide ranging, covering areas such as provision for the following:

- trade union recognition and collective bargaining in businesses of 21 or more employees
- extended powers for the Central Arbitration Committee
- additional duties for ACAS
- access to trade union representation in grievance and disciplinary matters for all employees
- protection for striking workers, under statutory rules
- qualifying period for exercising full employment rights of redress reduced from two years to one year
- extended rights for access to employment tribunals
- compensatory award for unfair dismissal raised significantly above the previous £12,000 limit to £50,000. Total awards were, and can still be, in excess of these amounts
- equal treatment for part-time employees
- family friendly policies to include: unpaid parental leave, unpaid time off for emergencies, increased maternity leave and childcare strategies.

Unions could assist workplaces in the effective implementation of these changes so that jobs may be sustained. One way the unions could help is by working with individual businesses and to raise the awareness of national policymakers for business support services. Employers may require guidance on the processes and potential value of workplace representation as managers in companies started since 1980, particularly in new industry sectors, may have little background or understanding of the procedures now stipulated for collective representation, in the Employment Relations Act.

The Act is quite daunting to a person who has not been involved in workplace representation.[9] Conversely, newer trade union officials are less likely to have had experience of joint working exercises, where techniques, such as work measurement and job evaluation are directed at improving productivity and equitable payment-reward.

Other ways in which trade unions could assist practically in encouraging real employment opportunities in a market economy include:

- ensuring that informal learning is valued as well as learning that leads to qualifications and awards
- ensuring that employers are aware of any financial assistance that may be generally available, to adapt facilities to help those with a specific disability
- ensuring that basic skills initiatives include language assistance, as appropriate, for those work colleagues whose first written language is not English
- lobbying for further development of workplace learning especially in regard to NVQ level 3, so that barriers to apprenticeships and other training schemes for younger people are reduced.

The success of the legislation listed above, will partly depend upon unions now considering what new skills to bring to the negotiating table, so that they may enter into partnership agreements with employers that are effective for all those within the partnership's influence.

Good practice techniques

7 Marketing and managing services

Developing and maintaining a good reputation with SMEs is dependent on effective marketing and management of these services.

Measuring improvement in working with SMEs

To ensure that investment in marketing is capitalised upon and that improvements in work with SMEs can be gauged, a way of measuring such work should be determined. The measurements chosen may vary but they should have a logical base and be chosen before deciding what to continue marketing to small businesses.

Careful management of marketing activity carried out by college business development units or marketing departments has to be maintained, e.g. in terms of well-budgeted resources 'input' to achieve an acceptable series of 'outputs'. Some work is common to nearly all organisations, but colleges' work is complicated by additional inputs and outputs specific to their sector. The inputs common to all organisations include:

- market research, and the evaluation or development of core products and services
- marketing of services
- the recruitment, training and retention of appropriately skilled staff
- establish and maintain suitable premises.

Colleges may also undertake some of the following additional inputs:

- developing relationships between the college and its local small businesses[10]
- challenging negative perceptions of the college (if they exist) in the local business community
- stimulating the demand for learning
- establishing an awareness of the need to develop services to SMEs across the college.

Examples of common outputs include:

- delivery of services to SMEs
- a good local reputation, perhaps measured in terms of repeat business or recommending the college to others.

However, colleges' marketing activity may also be required to achieve additional longer-term outputs including:

- recruiting new learners from the workplace for the college's core courses. Sourcing work-placements for core students
- increasing the opportunity for core students' future employment, on completion of their studies
- increasing the number of relationships with business, so that there is greater opportunity to find new governors or sponsors, or other forms of partnership activity between those in education and business.

Details of what is on offer

Clarity is paramount when marketing support services to small businesses. Providers should ensure that it is clear:

- who is selling what (i.e. learning services) to whom (i.e. small workplaces) and why?
- how, when and for how long, where and at what price?

The SME clients need to see added advantage in terms of improved business performance, or in the reduction of risks associated with the business (see Appendix). Risks may relate, for instance, to effective implementation of new regulations without recourse to job loss, to the evaluation of some potential purchases or, simply, in reducing feelings of isolation.

Much good work focuses on the second set of questions above. To be able to answer 'how' the learners are anticipated to learn, colleges and many other developers of learning materials have spent much effort on designing their materials. Flexible ways of enabling small businesses' representatives to access training continue to be developed, e.g. in the evening and weekends, in learning centres and on employers premises to accommodate shift work.

Who is offering services?

SMEs need to be clear who is offering them services. Services may be offered by a college, either as an individual organisation, or as the lead body in a collaborative partnership and it is important that the business client knows who holds responsibility for the service and that there is consistency in this.

If the provider is well established and has a good local reputation, potential customers will find it much easier to think about purchasing services from it. Good reputation takes a long time to build and can be easily lost.

The potential customer will need to be satisfied that those delivering the services are willing and able to gauge where a referral to other areas of expertise should be made, to retain a good level of service. For instance, in the case of a college providing services, it may be in the best interest of the customer in the small workplace to refer them to:

- another member of college staff
- advice from responsible bodies and national helplines, in regard to regulation
- assistance from another public or privately funded service
- NTOs and awarding bodies for assistance, as appropriate to standards and to qualification-related issues.

Reputation can be enhanced by such referrals as the primary provider draws upon the available services to ensure that local small businesses receive the most practical and appropriate assistance. The decision to make a referral can be increasingly difficult if the primary provider feels under pressure to generate income by selling only their own organisation's training and development provision. On the other hand, making referrals demonstrates high ethical standards and can make good commercial sense for providers, as it avoids the expense of developing one-off services. Referrals can be good for all parties: unnecessary expense is saved, the secondary provider gains additional business providing tried and tested services, and the small businesses gain a more appropriate and comprehensive learning experience.

What services are being offered?

Learning services can incorporate many different forms of support. Colleges can aim to provide local small businesses directly or indirectly with:

- management of learning centres, on and off campus, so that community facilities are available to those from small businesses
- provision of helplines
- provision of speakers at local schools, to raise awareness of local job and apprenticeship opportunities
- supervision and co-ordination of staff who have been released to study on the training provider's premises
- vetting small businesses, prior to their provision of student placements on their premises, followed by management of such placements, with adequate briefing of parties prior to the placement, supervision of parties during the placement, and provision of adequate feedback after the placement
- providing taster sessions
- hosting meetings to keep in contact with local businesses
- assist SMEs with evaluation of different learning services, diagnostic or training needs analysis services
- mentoring of work-based learners
- support for NVQ requirements, e.g. supporting trainee assessors from the workplace, as required for NVQ level 3 and above
- guidance for mentors appointed from within the learner's workplace
- technical advice to support the learning process, e.g. to resolve a computer hardware problem or enable a learner to access courseware or other computerised learning materials
- delivery of teaching and tutorial work
- assessment, examination and moderation of courses
- New service specification and design, evaluation of available packages to the required design and development of new service provision.

The business coach

A comprehensive term for the all-inclusive role described above could be the Business Coach. The role needs to be all inclusive because no one, including the small business owner-manager, has in-depth knowledge of all the issues which may need to be addressed. The firm may call for assistance on any one of a wide series of issues, and the Business Coach has to be able to respond effectively. In a purely commercial environment the co-ordination part of the Coach role might need a clear 'referral' element, so that there was no motivation to cling to the work.

In addition to the tasks above, the representatives who deliver services to small businesses need to be able to gauge where to make a referral. In a college providing services they might refer to:

- another college member of staff
- regulatory bodies and national helplines
- Business Links or Small Business Service or services from appropriate commercial providers
- national training organisations and awarding bodies for assistance, as appropriate to standards and to qualification-related issues.

By making such referrals, the provider draws on all the potential services and the local small businesses receive the most practical and appropriate assistance. Such referrals make good commercial sense; for providers they avoid the expense of developing one-off services and so unnecessary expense is saved and small businesses get better assistance.

8 Identifying needs of SMEs

Gathering the views of small businesses on their development needs is crucial to determining ways in which learning and support services can help them to sustain and improve their performance levels. Views need to be gathered regularly and the knowledge gained used within a periodic review of the services marketed to them.
Views can be gathered on many aspects:

- in relation to things outside the business, like measuring the effectiveness of local, regional and national business support, and the impact of local authority planning processes on local, sustainable development
- in relation to the internal workings of small businesses, within their own strategic and operational aspects (see Appendix).

Views may be gathered through local employer liaison groups and in consultation with local businesses and strategic partners. Other good, impartial sources of local information can include summary details of small businesses enquiries to helplines, including those run by their trade and professional bodies. An increasing number of membership organisations do not have the resources to analyse and publish details, so that invaluable current information can remain unused. Impartial sources of small businesses' views should also be considered.[11]

Surveys and diagnostic packages

Surveys and diagnostic packages are two more ways of gathering information about small businesses' needs.[12] However, small businesses need good reasons to respond to surveys and access diagnostic packages, especially as there is an increasingly large number of surveys these days. Reasons can vary from helping individual businesses to determine areas where resources could be better used (see Appendix), through to helping participating businesses receive information in regard to specific markets.

To ensure that effective information is fed back to participating businesses, it is best to consult with small businesses or their trade bodies in regard to questionnaire and package design.

Many EU-funded projects have set out to develop a paper-based or computerised diagnostic package, but few seem to have succeeded in completing the packages and making them generally available after the end of their funding periods. Perhaps this can be addressed, along with that of the many survey questionnaires and other packages, by reference to the following:

- Surveys and diagnostic packages should set out to determine what practical assistance would help businesses, consistent with improving the company's business performance.

- Generally, questionnaires should not focus on single issues, like computer-related ones, and omit to ask practical, basic questions to solicit information about the actual problems being faced.

- Surveys should avoid using jargon or technical language, as not all small businesses employ training and personnel specialists who can interpret the jargon of learning services or be aware of the latest changes in educational and funding policies.

- Surveys need to enable the user to relate questions to his or her own situation and to gather some feedback based on the answers given.

- Packages and survey questionnaires should be impartial, not written in a way that slants the user towards a certain conclusion, e.g. a common fault is intimating that training needs *will* be identified, rather than *may* be identified. Reference to training and learning services should not be forced; the need for these and other support services must arise naturally, as the user determines his or her own needs in terms of areas requiring improvement of business performance. If such areas are identified, learning services provided from outside the business may be able to lead to some improvement.

- Package and questionnaire design must clearly specify the necessary level of assistance that is to be provided when the questionnaires are to be completed or the packages used. If a business support representative is always to be present during completion, then that person needs to have the skills to motivate use of the package or completion of the survey, and to help relate the questions to the small business's particular situation. Diagnostic packages and survey questionnaires must be robust, straightforward and motivational to use, if small businesses are to work through them with no assistance.

When used correctly, surveys and diagnostic packages can help SMEs develop thoughts and ideas, as well as reduce feelings of isolation. However, such questioning can form a major problem area, as business confidence is crucial, and great sensitivity to confidentiality and requests for financial information is required. There are two different target audiences for diagnostic packages:

- those who are setting up in business
- those who are reviewing their ongoing work for some reason, such as to alter its status from being non-incorporated into being incorporated, to add new product lines or services, or to plan for expansion.

Small businesses review their work either on an occasional or periodic basis, say monthly, quarterly or annually. This is done to seek productivity improvement, by better use of resources in some strategic or operational aspects (see Appendix) of their work. Perhaps a way to stimulate use of a diagnostic package is to attract a business to review its work over a trading period that it does not usually consider, e.g. if it enabled trends to be considered over a six-month trading period. Others may be motivated to use a diagnostic package to plan if they wish to:

- avoid the risk of non-conformance to current or changing legal and employment requirements, or to maintain a licence to trade
- enable the directors and owner-managers to delegate tasks as the business expands or changes, or perhaps as contingency planning, in case key workers become ill or leave, or as part of a planned exit strategy, to sell the business or as part of its succession planning.

One benefit of using a diagnostic package can be the added value found in comparing profitability of work, by different groups of products and services, or by different target markets. To counter the risk of a business's income from its main products and services dwindling, they may market those products and services in different ways, to different target groups, and may also diversify into other services. For instance, hoteliers may sustain most of their income by marketing business hospitality through national trade and professional magazines, but have a sideline in selling weekend breaks to a relatively local leisure market.

Surveying small businesses

Before carrying out a survey, providers must themselves be clear why they are doing it and that it relates to the improvement of their services to business. It must be clear to the small businesses' representatives why the survey is being undertaken.

Those being surveyed may identify elements where training or other support could be beneficial, or perhaps suggest ways in which local provision to local workplaces could be improved. If the businesses are surveyed initially and again six months later, positive changes in survey responses could indicate improvements, e.g. easier trading conditions or improved training and support services, due to effective action on prompt analysis of the initial survey's findings.

Small businesses could be chosen randomly for surveying purposes. This, along with objectivity when filling in the questionnaires, may ensure more reliable analysis of small businesses' views. Their details should be held in confidence, taking care that no employer or organisation is identified by name if publishing the findings.

It can take great effort to encourage response in postal surveys. It may be more effective to have in-depth interviews with a representative group of small businesses rather than sending them out at random. The in-depth approach allows the interview to be appropriately recorded, as long as the person being interviewed agrees. The in-depth approach can also be more fruitful, as any major problems can be raised during the process of gathering their views.

The survey process can assist those being surveyed, by encouraging them to look back on practical details over a recent trading period, such as:

- ways in which they could have been better organised, to have been more productive (for the strategic and operational aspects, see Appendix)
- where business improvements were made during the period, by seeking assistance from outside their businesses
- with hindsight, to acknowledge to themselves where outside assistance would have helped if it had been available and taken up.

Setting the questions

The ideal questionnaire is one designed for use during a structured interview, by the interviewer of the small business. Further invaluable information could be gained, for example, by recording the interview, but it would be imperative that both parties agree to this.

However, if resources do not permit one-to-one discussions with small businesses, then the same questions can be carried out by a postal or telephone survey. Where a questionnaire is designed initially for a postal survey, and then developed for telephone, group and face-to-face interviews, each form of the questionnaire needs to solicit the same core information, so that findings can be analysed systematically and fair comparisons made.

The first part of the questionnaire may focus on gathering information, which would assist supporters of small businesses, by questioning on the following topics:

- What is the nature of the business? What are the current staffing levels? How long has the business been trading? How many previous owners? Have you run a business before? Did the earlier business remain in your control, or has it been closed down, sold, bought out, merged within another business? Is your current business less or more profitable compared with two years ago? Do you feel that your trading levels will improve, deteriorate or remain the same in the next one or two years?

- Are you interested in free advice/training or using IT to develop aspects of your business? If so, what are the most convenient times to receive such advice/training? What is the preferred location and duration of such sessions?

- Do you currently use computerised technology? e.g. for word processing functions, invoicing, stock control, accounting or other functions. If not, are there any particular reasons for not using it, e.g. have they encountered difficulties in gaining impartial advice?

- Suggest ways in which your views could be taken forward within local economic regeneration work?

- What is your involvement with local larger businesses and in local networks and business associations?

- What is your take-up of locally delivered, state-instigated business support?

This set of questions may determine take-up in categories, including: management techniques, business planning, marketing/sales, customer services, financial management, import/export, and IT training. Such categories may be subdivided into a list relating to the training and support of the business owner/manager and into a duplicate list relating to training and support specifically for employees.

As appropriate, the following general questions may also be asked:

- What is the status of your organisation, e.g. a limited company, a charity, a community organisation limited by guarantee or a co-operative?
- Can your organisation call upon the resources of a larger one: perhaps a key client?
- What products and services do your particular organisation offer and which sector does it trade in? Do you usually sell to other organisations or direct to the public?
- How many years has your organisation been established?
- Is your organisation already in contact with an FE college? If so, describe shared activities (e.g. use of computer facilities, staff on day or block release, ad-hoc training and so on).
- Do you have reservations about contact with your local FE college? If so, why?
- Do you have reservations about contact with your local Business Link or Enterprise Agency? If so, why?
- How many full-time and part-time staff work in your organisation currently? Does your organisation have the same staffing levels and hours as it did about this time last year, including seasonal staff? If your answer is 'Yes', have the hours worked changed in any way? If your answer is 'No', please give the changes in full-time and part-time staffing levels.

The second part of the questionnaire would comprise questions that aim to determine small businesses' current views, so that locally available services are effective by being based on current knowledge of what would assist in protecting business viability and local jobs. A list of potential questions is provided in the Appendix.

All survey questionnaires may allow those surveyed to make any additional comment and to have the option of either remaining anonymous, or providing their organisation's name, with a contact name and telephone number. Lastly, the date the questionnaire was completed needs to be noted, and those surveyed should receive thanks for their co-operation.

9 Designing new services for SMEs

New services for small businesses include a wide range
of activities. In general terms these may include:

- raising awareness of specific regulatory requirements
- helping provide the management techniques and expertise
  to implement statutory requirements effectively
- implementing and interpreting a national initiative locally
- combining a series of national initiatives, into more focused and
  practical local services, e.g. an initiative to encourage a person to
  use a computer can be combined with the initiative that aims to
  raise his or her basic skill level, such as numeracy or literacy
- responding to current and anticipated needs of small businesses.[13]

The following services do not seem to be widely available:

- help to organise a job, conform to changing employment law and
  to health and safety requirements so that each member of staff
  has a fair work schedule and remuneration, consistent with
  law and the organisation's profitability[14]
- help to evaluate training services. This service would help
  the understanding of terminology used in learning services.
  It would help in gauging benefits of proposed formal and informal
  training services, and of associated costs of proposed formal
  assessments. It would help in estimating any preparation
  costs of a workplace assessor, particularly for evaluation
  of work-based training services which will lead to NVQs
- help to define computer requirements,
  including the regulatory aspects
- aid in impartial evaluation of available computerised
  facilities, in terms of anticipated and measured
  improvement in business performance.

When specifying learning opportunities through formal training
it is important to consider the needs of both the employer and the
learner. In addition to the usual ways of specifying learning services,

by deciding learners' objectives through setting learning outcomes and appropriate assessment criteria, services for the workplace need to relate to a specific objective for business improvement. This improvement could be in strategic or operational terms (see Appendix) but it is essential that the business benefit is articulated to secure the commitment of time and resources from all those involved in the workplace.

Learning that includes formal assessment involves additional cost. These may be direct financial costs or in terms of resources, where a workplace representative has to gain understanding of the assessment processes and make assessments. The added value of awards must be accepted by potential learners and also by their current employers to prove that it is in both their interests to fund additional costs of assessments.

Focusing initiatives to encourage small businesses to use ICT

Perhaps one of the most useful services is to be imaginative in combining high-profile initiatives, especially those current ones that relate to the use of computers.

There are many official initiatives that aim to encourage organisations to improve their use of ICT. For instance, e-business, e-commerce and e-learning directly encourage the use of ICT in workplaces, and lifelong learning encourages those in small workplaces to learn about computer facilities and to avail themselves of training and education services, which may be delivered using computerised facilities.

All these and other initiatives targeting workplaces should be co-ordinated in a rational way, so that initiative overload is avoided, both for those set to deliver initiatives and for those receiving the information and support. Although the objective of each initiative needs to be met, the combined effect needs to be beneficial, in terms of improved workplace performance and in developing competitiveness.

For success in small workplaces, each initiative should provide impartial advice and use terms that are practical, readily understood and well defined. The terms e-business, e-commerce and e-learning, for example, lack clear definition. Sometimes e-commerce covers the communication between business and consumers who are individuals, whereas e-business covers the communications between businesses or between official bodies and business. However, e-business can also be used to spur an organisation to improve its internal practices, by incorporating latest technology.

The delivery of learning materials and assessment on the internet is known as e-learning, but it can also incorporate an element of e-commerce, in that educational establishments may need to charge for their services. Developers of online educational processes may also require a charge to be made by users of e-learning facilities. Such charges may be the only way for developers and publishers to recoup their initial development investment costs. It also provides them with funds for further development, and to support their products during early integration by teaching staff into courses.

Effective work-based computer-related learning

Addressing the issues of rights, security and contract law

E-business, e-commerce and e-learning raise issues which need to be addressed through development of effective learning services to small businesses. Irrespective of how these terms are defined, they can share problem areas, including those relating to rights, in data protection, in copying and in authorship of materials, and in licensing of software application packages. E-business, e-commerce and e-learning can also all involve use of the internet, to transfer or retrieve information online, and require a high level of security for their key transactions. The security of online transaction details relies on an effective system of encoding programmes. Such programmes generate scrambling software which is used in many things, from mobile telephones to internet browsers. The programmes protect transactions involving credit card and order details, and also transactions which record students' use of e-learning materials and of online assessments of students' work.

Countries which try to police the encoding programmes, for instance, to monitor transactions for state purposes, meet the problem that the internet takes no notice of national or trading block boundaries. In Europe, business representatives, consumer organisations and regulatory authorities meet to sort the vexed questions of legal competence and the application of trade and contract laws to e-commerce; sorting the conflicts of jurisdiction and provision of contract law, and the subsequent influence on the protection of consumer rights. The decision on where an internet commercial transaction is deemed to have taken place has been debated at length within the European Union. As at the start of 2000, no legal basis exists in which everyone has confidence. It may be that no satisfactory position can be achieved, until global agreement on legal and security issues is gained.

Those wishing to use the internet for commercial transactions need to be well aware of this lack of resolution on the legal and security aspects. It is certainly the responsibility of those set to stimulate organisations to use the internet in this way, to ensure they understand the very real risks currently involved.

Retaining existing good administrative practice

E-commerce and e-business involve processes where organisations automate their administrative systems' functions to improve performance in some way. All organisations have administrative systems maintained on a computer, whether they are sales order processing systems or teaching timetables. Newly introduced computerisation may directly replace manual processes, or extend processes, e.g. to enable the organisation to use the internet to market itself and to sell its services to a broader community. Unfortunately, organisations can forget some good, basic practices when they start implementing new computer facilities. If an organisation finds a new customer from abroad, through using the internet, it still needs to check their credit worthiness. Likewise, if a new supplier is found through using the internet, the organisation still needs to agree the purchase price and delivery requirements, and still undertakes a risk in purchasing from that new source. A key difference in buying or selling using the internet, is that organisations may be entering, for the first time, into relationships with customers or suppliers who are based abroad, who trade under different legal systems and with different business traditions.

Appropriate materials

The pitfalls specific to e-learning relate to integrating computerised facilities successfully into a student's course and being able to assess the contribution of the integrated part to that of the whole. Successful implementation of e-learning facilities lies in the early recognition that many do not allow teaching and training staff to create their own materials; only a few e-learning tools have been designed to allow staff to generate resources which incorporate their own materials. Teaching staff may well find their own materials easier to implement, and avoid major revision of courses. Also, many such facilities are library resources; although these may be attractive to users, as they incorporate good visual and aural functionality, the assessment of their effective use often relies on processes which are outside the library resources. On the other hand, the type of e-learning process which comprises a series of linear texts, interspersed with groups of exercises, can be easier to integrate into courses, as the exercises form inbuilt tests the student's understanding. However, the inbuilt assessment processes can greatly increase the cost of developing such e-learning packages.

Motivations for using e-learning, e-commerce and e-business

The motivation for ensuring the effective design and implementation of e-commerce, e-business and e-learning processes may all be the same, in that organisations contract or employ staff specifically to undertake such tasks on their behalf. This motivation, to fulfil one's contract of employment, also applies to those who have jobs that utilise e-commerce and e-business processes. However, the motivation required to use e-learning processes are very different.

In an ideal world, students using e-learning facilities would be driven by interest, consulting e-learning facilities as they might consult materials in a conventional library. This ideal relies on the intrinsic interest generated by the use of multimedia resources, the aesthetic appeal of such resources and the pleasure of using them, the concentration of relevant material in single resources, and the obvious relevance of those resources to the student's course of action. In practice, students usually have to be stimulated to access e-learning. Such stimulation may be for course assessment purposes, where the onus is placed on the student to consult some e-learning facilities to complete a piece of work which is then assessed. Another stimulation can be for reference purposes, as a main source of information which is stipulated during lectures and seminars. Both types of stimulation require teaching staff to have gained considerable familiarity with the e-learning facilities and to have thought carefully about when to refer to them during lectures and seminars, so that students understand the relevance of using the e-learning processes.

Benefits of implementing computerised facilities

The benefits of implementing new computer facilities, whether in the name of e-commerce or e-business, are gained by the improvement in organisational performance and control, through achieving better working conditions for the organisation's staff and in the potential broadening of its trading activities. The benefits of implementing e-learning in an organisation are the same, in that effective e-learning will improve the use of an organisation's investment resources or reduce the risks of trading, as employees are better prepared to do their jobs.

A possible benefit of e-learning to publicly funded provision is to refine or change the way that the education and training budget is used to promote the take-up of learning by people in the workplace. E-learning facilities can reap the following benefits:

- make more effective use of teaching staff, e.g. using ICT in routine areas of introductory courses, and so effectively deal with increasing student numbers and higher staff-to-student ratios

- reduce the need for supervisory staff involvement in organisations that wish to train or educate their own staff. The e-learning processes, as with e-commerce ones, are successful when they enable business or organisational performance to be improved, or be sustained through increasing resources for productive work, thus enabling time spent on supervisory, research or instructive tasks to be better used.

- enable learning to be organised on a more flexible basis, by allowing learners to progress at their own speed and repeat sections of courses as required. E-learning can be very effective in addressing remedial teaching and learning.

The costs of implementing e-commerce, e-business and e-learning facilities must be weighed against the benefits so that the net improvement in competitiveness can be gauged. Potential costs can include the following:

- purchasing and installation of computer hardware and of software facilities, and considered planning for their ongoing maintenance, security and access aspects

- ensuring that the rights of developers, distributors and authors are understood, with proper consideration of commercial aspects, e.g. licences for use and licences for commercial exploitation of newly developed facilities

- planning the implementation of new facilities, by allocating appropriate time and other resources for authors and developers, and for those who will implement and use the new facilities. Tasks may include: the production of learning materials, the specification and design of facilities, and the changes required to daily work to integrate the new facilities, so that benefits of integration are gained from early phases of implementation

- making adjustments to daily work routines, e.g. in current teaching timetables or in organisational aspects, to make best use of the new facilities

- arranging and providing technical support for users of new facilities, including sessions to raise awareness of how to use the facilities and how to conform to ancillary requirements, e.g. for security or housekeeping purposes.

10 Forging partnerships

Creating bridges between education and industry is vital to the national economy. Partnership activity can take many forms, and may not always be directly related to provision of training. Indeed, the simple supplier/provider relationship which is found when a college provides a given service or training course for an employer at full cost to the employer, is somewhat different from the sustained partnership arrangements between education and industry which may reap more substantial benefits.[15]

SMEs are more difficult to involve in strategic partnerships, as their resources are already strained in maintaining their business. However, the increasing percentage of SMEs in the profile of businesses nationally means that they cannot be excluded from such partnership activity. FE providers have a great deal of intellectual capital that could be of value to SMEs. There is potential for joint research and problem solving which could be extremely useful to small businesses and provided locally, more quickly and less expensively than commercial or HE supplied services.

Many publicly funded initiatives have aimed over many years, to stimulate and co-ordinate different forms of partnership between education and business. Some, such as the Education Business Partnerships (EBPs), have attempted to bring together the various interested parties, including employers, teaching staff, careers advisers, government-funded organisations, as well as students.

Activities have included the following:

- work experience placements, for students, teaching and lecturing staff
- schemes to raise the profile of career opportunities in specific sectors, including liaison between colleges and schools, presentations by employers, and participation by individuals within schemes like the Neighbourhood Engineer
- the establishment of community facilities, e.g. by colleges providing small, local businesses with access to computers and the internet, and other services

- schemes to raise awareness of business and work issues within educational establishments, including involvement of business people as mentors to pupils on Young Enterprise projects, and as mock interview panel members.

However, key factors militate against forging effective partnerships:

- Partnership co-ordination agencies may receive only short-term funding, and have faced a series of frequent, major reorganisations during the last twenty years.
- The potentially confusing variety of different partnership initiatives has been a major factor in many either not becoming established or not having gained credence with workplace partners. Poorly funded and inadequately managed initiatives may have resulted in an overlap of organisations trying to stimulate the same activities with the same target audience. Overlap also occurs when initiatives, like those in computing or engineering, are instigated by the government and also by trade associations and professional bodies.
- Those from the workplace have found it very difficult to become involved, due to constraints on their time and resources. A further barrier to partnership for many potential workplace partners arises from the lack of a commonly understood language by the education industry.
- Although local and regional registers are already maintained by central co-ordinating bodies, they often cover only a subset of the many different partnership activities. Consequently, local workplaces can be approached by different co-ordination bodies, asking for involvement in different activities. This is ineffective for large workplaces, and detrimental to small workplaces.
- The development of partnerships is patchy. There are still regions of England and Wales where local employers are not aware of practical details of the courses and other workplace services that their local providers offer for specific industry sectors. This lack of awareness makes the job of generating take-up of learning or involvement in development activity more difficult.

Defining the benefits to the workplace

Expanding economic activity, recruiting new staff, and bringing in new staff for the long term can all be strong motivations to work in partnership with local educational establishments. Enabling businesses to recruit locally, through their partnership work with local educational establishments, is also a key incentive to those in education to plan their partnerships more imaginatively and efficiently.

However, this involvement depends upon them having a better idea of the resources and levels of commitment available from current or potential partners in the workplace.

Partners in the workplace will only willingly come forward to help if the needs of the schools, colleges and universities are clearly and concisely defined in the first place, and if only reasonable demands are made on their resources. Those who do become involved in partnership activities may withdraw if they experience a lack of proper co-ordination or support, e.g. if college staff fail to monitor their students properly while on work placement.

Many workplaces have little time to spare for resourcing partnership activities with local educational bodies, as they continue to trade in difficult and uncertain commercial conditions. Likewise, those in education face many significant changes, including budget cuts and in curricula. This leaves their staff with less time to think about and plan activities involving members of the local working community, that could benefit all concerned.

There must be tangible benefits to the business of SMEs entering into partnership activities. This is only achieved if each activity is properly specified and 'sold' to those in the workplace. A formal specification could be produced to determine the objectives for the overall business and for each participant.

Reconciling conflicting agendas

It should be recognised that the objectives of education and of business may conflict, particularly where this concerns the provision of work placements for students. The responsibility for resolving such conflicts, amicably and quickly with all parties concerned, has to lie with the provider. The college must be able to communicate with the employer, and try to ensure that all parties gain from the activity.

Partnership activities can easily fail, with the consequent loss of interest in being involved in any future partnership activities.

Short-term versus long-term benefits

A key reason for a lack of involvement by businesses when it comes to training staff is that activities have been instigated to achieve long-term objectives and the company is more concerned with short-term priorities. For example, activities that:

- have the objective of educating businesses, by promoting a 'learning culture' set out to address difficult remedial issues, including some workers' relatively low levels of literacy and numeracy

- gather businesses' views to achieve change, perhaps in the way that a region determines the potential career opportunities by industry sector, or to feed back to national bodies, e.g. to NTOs, for the reform of key industry training standards
- aim to achieve cultural changes, perhaps to stimulate collaboration between a region's educational establishments or between business support providers in a region.

Such activities may well be fundamental for the long-term wealth of the nation and for much needed social cohesion, but partnership activities must also be designed to achieve short-term benefits for business partners. Unless this is the case, the time and resources needed for partnership activities may deflect attention from the firm's core business, thus current employment is jeopardised and business partners cannot risk becoming involved. Perhaps such activities, in the short term, should be used as incentives to business partners, and accompanied by a tax rebate or some other financial compensation, to encourage their involvement.

A register of services

A register of services available locally, regionally and nationally could alleviate some of the problems of working effectively with SMEs. It could provide information on:

- capacity to deliver training and offer services to SMEs
- partnership initiatives between education and business
- requirements for work placements or staff exchanges
- potential for joint research and problem solving

The register could include information about local providers and set out the business benefits of involvement. It could also include information about the local employment base, skills needs and profile of employers in the area.

A register would make the task of participation in learning by the workplace, and all other partners less demanding, by providing information to allow the managers/proprietors of businesses large and small, to evaluate the benefits of becoming involved. It would assist those in education to know what provision is offered locally. It would be valuable to partners already participating, and build on the work already achieved in a region. Partnership participation would be more likely, as the register could provide a 'one-stop-shop' for all partners, by providing a vehicle for pulling together information on many different partnership initiatives.

The register would be best maintained electronically and should be complemented by a simple booklet describing how the register works for both business and education partners. It would also provide an ideal place to acknowledge publicly the generosity of the workplaces that have undertaken partner activities. It could also include a report on local employers' comments, so that the organisation of future partnership activities could be made more effective.

This kind of booklet should be produced in close consultation with interested parties, like schools, business people, Young Enterprise, employers and individuals. The booklet would be informative and serve to advertise the register and detailed activities to current and potential partners. It could recognise and describe the essential input from any commercial organisations that wished to sponsor its publication.

Instigating and co-ordinating the register

The success of the register of services may depend upon its added value at regional or local level, perhaps within a specific set of industry sectors. Success also depends on the register being produced by a body able to communicate with potential business partners, as well as with senior staff in educational establishments. Consequently, instigating and maintaining the register, and producing a booklet, could give a sponsor a high regional or industry sector profile, with the following benefits:

- It could be used to encourage colleges in a region to produce a brochure of the services they offer workplaces in specific sectors, e.g. defence and aerospace, or perhaps a generic type of organisation, e.g. independently run organisations with fewer than 250 staff.
- It could form a specific initiative, or focal point, to advertise the sponsor's interest, and stimulate their own, core activities, e.g. a membership group from within the workplace could raise its profile, to gain further members, consistent with the ideals of the register.

Initial and ongoing costs

Sufficient resources to set up a register of services are crucial, whether they are completely financial or partly 'in-kind'. Resources for ongoing maintenance could be much less, organised to focus on periodic production of advertising material, including occasional reissue of an updated booklet, to keep stimulating activities at the required regional level. This may well be sufficient to sustain the momentum.

The establishment and ongoing maintenance of the project register would involve the following tasks:

- collaboration with local co-ordinators of services and partnership activities, to produce a booklet detailing how the register would work locally

- search and specification of new activities. This could be assisted by circulation of the booklet to local education establishments, local employers or county and regional organisations. The booklet, or a periodic newsletter, could be a major way to disseminate details of successful partnership activities achieved and so stimulate new activities. The documentation circulated could be self-financing, from income generated by sale of advertising or sponsorship

- putting additional details on to the register, giving clear objectives, so that each of the partners can gauge the benefits to them of becoming involved, and then illustrate and sell those benefits to their staff and students

- generating partner interest in specific activities, by selling specific activities from the register

- analysing the benefits gained by partners on completion of each activity, learning from activities which have failed to produce adequate benefits for all the parties involved, and noting success stories to use in the booklet or newsletter.

Information on how to run successful services, training or partnership activities could be incorporated in the guidance booklet.

Appendix

Sample questions

This appendix should be read in conjunction with the good practices above, when gathering the views of small businesses on their development needs. The good practice on gathering these views provides many of the general questions that may be asked of them, to complement the following questions, which are at strategic or operational levels.

When colleges are assisting businesses in evaluation of services, the small business has to judge if benefits could be gained at the overall, strategic level, as well as at the level of operational tasks. The following questions can act as an aide memoire during such evaluation processes. For each question, the activity being assessed needs either to:

- reduce the small business's input, to enable it to improve the use of its current resources, or reduce sources of worry and risk

  or to:

- increase the amount that the small business can output, from the current level of resources.

  Also, under certain market conditions, services being evaluated may provide the opportunity to:

- increase both inputs and outputs to enable expansion.

Advice on using the questionnaire

The questions listed below should only be used as a bank from which providers can draw upon, rather than a 'set' of questions to be kept together.

The purpose of the investigation, and the business context, should provide the starting point, and topic areas should emerge from these. Where possible, it would be beneficial to approach SMEs in partnership with other key players, such as the SBS, as some of the information required may already have been gathered by them.

Some strategic-level questions

- Is the organisation's overall performance satisfying the owners' reasons for staying in business? If not, is the production of an exit strategy in hand or required, e.g. to close the business before a financial crisis occurs or to hand it over to a new owner-manager?

- Are there effective ways in which to reduce the organisation's costs of understanding and conforming to legal requirements?

- Is awareness of basic financial, work study, productivity and equitable payment-reward issues, adequate to ensure that sufficient internal systems are in place to control the business and to make it a fair place to work?

- Would a one-off efficiency exercise increase the chance of retaining a licence to trade, by enabling the organisation to be better able to prove its internal systems or qualification levels to regulatory or licensing authorities?

- Would a better focus on entry into new markets or better penetration of a current market be effective?

- Is the organisation's performance limited by a lack of delegation of key tasks, e.g. in case key workers become ill or leave, or to free the owner-manager from day-to-day operational tasks?

- Should the organisation look into ways of attracting new employees or achieving better retention of current staff, perhaps through design of valued apprenticeships?

Some operational-level questions

The detailed views of businesses need to be gathered on their key administration tasks. These are the indirect tasks, that are common to organisations across many sectors, and which can take a disproportionate amount of small organisations' resources. These common tasks are undertaken by an organisation to support the direct tasks that are specific to the production and delivery of each different organisation's business, product and service.

Even when surveys are customised not all questions will be relevant to every small businesses' trading activity. Survey forms and diagnostic packages need to ensure that a 'not applicable' answer can be recorded.

Where a business' response indicates specific tasks that are not going to plan, additional questions may be valuable:

- What is the level of concern arising from these tasks, in the range 1 to 5 (where, for instance, 1 is a low level, and 5 is a high level)?

- If the cause of concern is already being addressed:

– Did an external authority (e.g. a local enforcement agency and/or a state-funded, national helpline) provide information which eased this task? Did training by an external body (e.g. a college, or a private commercial training organisation) help to ease this task?

– Did an external adviser (e.g. a professional adviser, like an accountant who sells services on a commercial basis, a college mentor or an adviser from a Business Link) help to ease this task?

- With hindsight, would this task have been eased by 'some' or 'more' advice or information, in the last year?
- With hindsight, would 'some' or 'more' training have eased this task, in the last year?

The answers to the additional questions above, can be useful to reduce unnecessary duplication of local services. The thought that has to go into answering questions in hindsight, in effect, triggers a review of a specific aspect, year on year. This may well result in a realisation that certain aspects have become much harder or more expensive over the last twelve months, or that some aspect has improved over that period.

Some questions to highlight problem areas within indirect tasks

- Have you spent more time and/or money in marketing the organisation and what it offers, and in monitoring competitors?
- Have you needed to change the status of your organisation, e.g. from charitable status to incorporated status?
- Have you had difficulty in securing new contracts to supply other organisations?
- Have you spent time in leasing premises or in achieving appropriate planning permission?
- Has extra time been spent in applying new employment regulations?
- Has extra time been spent in applying health and safety requirements?
- Has extra time been spent in gathering and collating details for tax return and trading account purposes?
- Have your standard sales terms needed to be revised or service levels reduced due to reducing trade?
- Has extra time been spent on financial issues, debt chasing or revising expenditure plans?
- Has extra time and/or money been spent in getting relevant export documentation?
- Has extra time been spent in understanding management standards, like ISO 9000 or the Investors in People Award?
- Has extra time been spent carrying out audits or assessments?
- Has extra time been spent on the selection or installation of computer facilities?
- Do staff consistently need to work outside normal hours?
- Has extra time been spent due to unanticipated staff turnover and/or recruitment difficulties?
- Has extra time been spent trying to find information and assistance that are specific to your type of work?

Questions to highlight problem areas within direct tasks

- If the performing of indirect tasks were less time-consuming (see above), would the time saved be put to good use on direct tasks?
- Has your organisation had training on the tasks directly concerned with the production of its products and services in the last year?
- Has your organisation had assistance via the SBS on the production or delivery of its products and services in the last year?
- Has your organisation sought advice or information from a specialist, non-state funded, commercial supplier on the tasks directly concerned with the production or delivery of its products and services in the last year?
- Has your organisation had assistance in improving real and sustainable profit and productivity levels in the last year?
- With hindsight, would additional training on direct tasks over the last year have been helpful in protecting jobs or expanding the organisation?
- With hindsight, would your organisation have benefited from additional advice or information in relation to the tasks directly concerned with the production of its products and services in the last year?

References

1   Coffield F. *Breaking the consensus: lifelong learning as social control.* Inaugural lecture, Department of Education, University of Newcastle, 1999.

2   Department of Trade and Industry, 1998. 99.8% of UK businesses are businesses with up to 250 staff; 55% of the employment in UK businesses is provided by those with up to 250 staff

3   Third report of the National Skills Task Force, Tackling the adult skills gap: upskilling adults and the role of workplace learning, DfEE, 2000.

4   Office of National Statistics, for period February–April 2000.

5   Teaching and Higher Education Act 1998, Part III *Right to time off for study or training*, 1999. This sample legislation has guidance that directs employers towards the National Training Organisations' National Council, for their redirection to 'the NTO for a specific sector'. A list of over 90 specified qualification awarding bodies for the regulations is also provided. Such guidance examples the daunting research and evaluation tasks for most employers and many colleges. This particular example is even more concerning, considering difficulties in evaluating training may well form a barrier to employers taking on young staff. Website: www.dfee.gov.uk/tfst.htm

6   FEDA/Association of Colleges. *Improving the value of NVQs and other vocational qualifications.* FEDA/AoC, 1999.

7   e.gov-electronic governance services for the 21st century performance and innovation unit. September 2000. Website: www.cabinetoffice.gov.uk/innovation/2000/delivery/indexFrame.htm

8   The guides – *Employing staff: a guide to regulatory requirements* (URN 99/933); *Setting up in business: a guide to regulatory requirements* (URN 99/833); and *Tendering for government contracts* (URN 99/1055) are obtainable via www.dti.gov.uk/publications/sme, Department of Trade and Industry, 1999.

9   *A better way to work*, TUC, 1997 – ISBN 1 85006 390 7. The five sections of this practical Educational Resource for Work Experience and Careers Education, ideally need to be extended to include a section to brief the potential employers of the future.

10 'Clustering' can now follow a strict methodology and incorporate recent philosophies (The Clusters Approach, SE/1542/MAR 98 [1998], Scottish Enterprise), but is used here in the sense of groupings which share common interests. A cluster of small businesses can have the common bond of, for example, serving the same customer or types of customer, facing a down-turn in business due to a particular local planning decision, or having purchased from the same computer software or course-ware supplier or training establishment. Clustering can also enable those within it to have market and economic information collated and shared jointly, to the mutual benefit of all concerned. This may also enable the cluster to share such information with those who have regional influence and at national and government levels, perhaps in conjunction with the Small Business Service.

11 The Quarterly Reports by the Small Business Research Trust have formed a practical source of small businesses' views since 1983 (see reference 2 above). Further impartial sources include: *Finance for smaller firms; a fifth report*, Bank of England, 1998, *SME finance and regulation: a survey from the Enterprise Group of the Institute of Chartered Accountants in England and Wales*, Institute of Chartered Accountants in England and Wales, 1999.

12 The project entitled 'Centre for enabling small and medium sized enterprises' (CESaME) received EU funds within the Leonardo Da Vinci programme, to lay the basis for developing a pan-European network of business coaches to support smaller businesses and to generate a database of information and training materials for smaller businesses and for business coaches. The Leonardo Da Vinci programme was curtailed, which caused CESaME's work to go into abeyance. CESaME's Associate Director (Materials Development), Mike Bolton has ensured that CESaME's ideas are taken forward, by informing the ADAPT FESME VCU project, and by working with colleagues to develop a diagnostic package. E-mail: mike.bolton@virgin.net

13 Pengelly RJ. *Progressive management of small firms: raising communities' prosperity*, 2000, A+K, ISBN 1 84108 003 9) provides policy-makers, smaller businesses and their supporters with a purchaser's view of the barriers faced by a large organisation that wishes to buy from smaller, local firms. This constructive list has practical checklists to aid those setting up or running small firms and those developing effective training and other services for the sector of smaller employers. The author may be contacted via: nweu@calemcal.demon.co.uk

14 An example resource to aid successful implementation of the Disability Discrimination Act 1995, is provided by the Careers Advisory Network on Disability Opportunities (CanDo), which advises employers, runs training courses and works with government, HE institutions, the media and disability organisations to promote better access to employment. CanDo can be contacted by e-mail: enquiries@cando.ac.uk Its web-based careers information resource for disabled students is available on www.cando.ac.uk

15 Learning and Skills Development Agency. Hughes M and Cottam S. *Partnership for skills*. 2000